SHEARSMAN

137 & 138

WINTER 2023 / 2024

EDITOR
TONY FRAZER

Shearsman magazine is published in the United Kingdom by
Shearsman Books Ltd
P.O. Box 4239
Swindon
SN3 9FL

Registered office: 30–31 St James Place, Mangotsfield, Bristol BS16 9JB
(this address not for correspondence)

www.shearsman.com

ISBN 978-1-84861-910-4
ISSN 0260-8049

Subscriptions and single copies

Current subscriptions – covering two double-issues, each around 100 pages in length –
cost £17 for delivery to UK addresses, £24 for the rest of Europe (including the Republic
of Ireland), £28 for Asia & North America, and £30 for Australia, New Zealand and
Singapore. Longer subscriptions may be had for a pro-rata higher payment. Purchasers
in North America and Australia will find that buying single copies from online retailers
there will be cheaper than subscribing, especially following recent drastic price-rises for
international mail. This is because copies are printed locally to meet such orders from
online retailers. Due to the changes in 2021 to the treatment of cross-border transactions
in the EU, purchasers in the EU (except for those in Ireland) are recommended to use
EU-based online retailers, although they can sometimes be a little slow to update their
databases for non-domestic publications.

Back issues from nº 63 onwards (uniform with this issue) cost £9.95 / $17 through retail
outlets. Single copies can be ordered for £9.95 direct from the press, post-free within the
UK, through the Shearsman Books online store, or from bookshops. Contact us regarding
earlier issues (i.e. nos. 1–62), whether for single copies or a complete run.

Submissions

Shearsman operates a submissions-window system, whereby submissions may only be made
during the months of March and September, when selections are made for the October and
April issues, respectively. Submissions may be sent by mail or email, but email attachments
are only accepted in PDF form. We aim to respond within 3 months of the window's closure,
although we do sometimes take a little longer.

Acknowledgements

This issue has been set in Arno Pro, with titling in Argumentum. The flyleaf is set in Trend Sans.

Contents

In memoriam

Gavin Selerie
1949–2023

and

Avik Chanda
1972–2023

Eliza O'Toole

Usual is wind from the east
(without struggle or fight, reaction to light, endogenous rhythms)

It was a machine gun of a morning, a
cock pheasant in a clamour of flight
and a woodpecker jack hammering.
The sky was green. It was astringent
and the blackthorn was wild and
white. It was the way the oak was
growing, narrowing the sky and
fracture pruned. It was stag headed
and rose over. The kites were cork
screwing, a pair, slowly circling way
up there. Fin was mesmerised. Then
it started to sleet, and there was a
vast inrolling of petals, and ice was in
the air. It was a capitulum of a closing
after the beginning of an opening,
it was loss of light intensity and
temperature drop. It was *aconitum
lycoctonum*, cowled and hooded,
ground hugging and glowing, bane
butter yellow spilling, arisen from a
mythological dog's vomiting.

the colours of pollen
(put pollen upon for the sake of fertilisation)

It was a vixen piss of a morning. Sour
scat of that. A brace of pink legged
partridge startle. Fin, scenting, nose
to the ground finds shreds of pelt,

scatterings of barbes and down, moults of winter coat windblown and then tiny white sharp shucked knuckles, links of vertebrae laid down slight covered in copper curls of last year's slow stuck wet dehiscing leaves. And in the blet scent of that Fin, rootling under the cherry plum, flushes a blackbird and they both jump, dusting a blush of brick red pollen brightly onto bone.

It was the way the light was falling
(unfastening, west of the horse shoe weir)

It faltered, a rainy river morning, gravid with sleet. And in the shul shul of the wind, black backed gulls were sliding. And in the fret and mute and the slap of that, a twisted thing. Hand, eye and Fin, bolt upright. In the seep and creep, the lifting and the withdrawing, a scuppering. Overwhelmed, strip barked, part skinned, eyes gone, sinews skeined. Plundered. Catched, coagulating, fractured branches, hedge whacked twigs, plastic sacking, renegate baling twine (blue), snare tight Alder root snatch ravelling rib bones and then unmooring. A pruning. Creely the riverbank, the colour of cold, it was the crows, the crows, the sky as thin as tin and in the sedge, Fin quivering.

Unearthed

(stræl, belonging to a bow, a splintering)

At dawn, a tawny owl was calling. It was that sort of morning. Fin was watching contrails split the sky. It was greening, a wild garlic of a morning, emerald and styptic white and the plough lines, pitch perfect, were reaching right into the sky.

It was the way the barley was breaking through, the way the barleybirds rose in a single motion, the way the moon was transparently there, like a marble in my mouth. And it was the way the field was overturned, belly sown with knuckles of bone, spicules of silicious stone, cortical dorsal and newly arisen. Fin was digging wriggling in the earth, warm brown musky aroma of dirt arced & showering. It was flicked up, hard hammer struck, then a chip and then a splinter, it was shot, it was lithic, and then it was an echo of a relic of an elf-arrow head.

Then ascending, it was the way the horizon was perched pigeon feather soft, fine bladed with flakes of cloud and squat colours of flint, scattered, and as our track ditched the burgage plot, there was strong green through old stone, and it was growing over.

In the cold, the air was thickening.

The closure of crocus

(Crocus is an example of a flower that closes when temperatures drop. Colour is withheld. Pollination too. The minimum decrease in temperature … [is] … about equal to the temperature rise required for opening.)

It was an owl call of a morning, cold and fay. Ice tipped rigid immobility, a white day.

Scare crows, it was a blæc death, it was a murder

~~*(as the crow flies)*~~

It was a shock. Not a gas gun stunning of the morning, raising riots of wood pigeons clap cracking & clacking, not warping our walking, not making us run. It was a sudden blow, we were shred and thrown, stopped fast and in the cleaving rain, we stood heaped as sheaves, one against the other. In a shock, still. It was feather dark, absorbing all the light, it was a sweart swinging thing. Blacker than Fin, and leaning in, he was shivering. And then there were rows. They were slight winging buffetings spread across the harrowed fields, they were striking, and, on the horizon, it was a slap and a punch, they were hanging there, swinging there, they were crucified there, they were spreadeagling and cable tied, fletching, gibbeting and wind-fidgeting there. They were strong-beaked and silent, they were scaring, they were sown and broken, and they had been grackle glossy black clever carrion crows.

Trevor Joyce

Harm's Way

For Bríd Walshe

i.m. Mary Lee (1872–1936)

1
even when I tried she said
the earth was stony and the food was foul

even when I spoke she said
my sense wasn't to be found in books

even when I sang she said
they didn't understand my airs

and when I drank she said
an ocean couldn't satisfy

then when I saw the spirit world
the doors slammed in their face

they called me troublesome destructive
dangerous turned me on myself

red blossoms gleam
beneath her nails

2
come child you should be with me
come away from the warmth

and the lime-washed darkness
with talk inside of it sweet

as the mauve flesh of a damson
there's a hunger in me

for the road and my child beside me
I am my own affliction

come bear with me my last
uneasiness my inability to

rest her blue shimmering eyes
flowers in an orchard of infirmity

Serena Alagappan

Bitter Like a Nightingale

Your fear feels like a well filled with saltwater
like snow flumping into rain on the pavement
like muddy walks uphill,
like a quilt of sea heaving in thunder,
a mouth with no teeth in a dream,
a myth with no elder to share it,
a mime with a pirate smile,
like a bouquet of embalmed lilies,
like a winter sweat from layers,
like a God of nothing dogma,
a miraculous birth many weeks early,
a wishbone during a boring dinner
with people you love, but will never tell,
like treating nihilism with the salve of hard
problems, like a wild flapping
of fingers on keys, like plans that can only
be rudely unmade, a falling for what
is out of our control, like joy and grief,
coconuts plucked clean of hair, meals served
on waxy leaves, time fattened in napping
afternoons, like one long braid with 6 strings
of jasmine, like 9 squirrels ravaging sweet
plums, like 7 kid cousins begetting children,
and me, 9 years later, reassuring that we will
be okay, that we are grown-ups who can make
grown-up decisions, like having dessert before
dinner, and keeping all our promises.

Her first time on the Bimah

was in the chapel of a Unitarian church,
and her granddaughter was being
Bat-mitzvahed, and her granddaughter
was brown, and most of the guests wore
saris. She stood up, (awkward? proud?)
and stepped closer to the Torah, where
her husband mumbled transliterations
of ancient Hebrew. Her auburn curls
formed a crown, a triskelion brooch
pinching her breast. Her hand wavered
as the Torah passed. She used her program
as mediator, touched it to the scroll, then
kissed the pointer's paper. She did not have
a complex about sitting with women in
a different section from men during Orthodox
services. She did not have a complex about
hearing the Shema in a Universalist sanctuary.

This was, of course, in her eighties. Perhaps our
complexes fade with age, like sand forgiving
the shatter of waves, like the refuge shore
of rocky coastline made from all that breakage.

Tread Softly

The god of death careens in the holes
Not bad holes, like stars shrill in the sky,
Not bad death, like Midas's goldbite.
Apparently, you know how much we
Love each other, though this is the first
I'm hearing. I'll hold her in Heaven's cloth,
Promise, and in your absence, though in
Your presence first, joy nears, posthumous birth.

Rupert M Loydell

The Critical Gaze

1. Comprehension

'The future has been over for a while.'
—Eugenio Montale

I've been finding it ever so difficult.
Fragmentary signals, isolated gestures,
cries and whispers all resist attempts
to unravel meaning. Back I go, pushing
and dragging phrases into patterns
which are then tested to destruction.

Making use of the found and discarded
is an important part of autobiography;
solitude not solidarity is the normal,
syntax is no longer in the driving seat,
no-one is named and names do not seem
to be attached to anyone in particular.

I find it difficult to escape repetition.
Theologians stress order and principle,
while philosophers maintain either that
life obeys some rules or that it does not.
But you're wondering what became of
comprehension, aren't you? Ghosts

soon begin speaking, explaining things.
Understand motivation and purpose
are only diversions, truth and desire
fall between reality and imagination.
Those who invent a recognisable past
legitimise only certain ways of seeing.

2. The Critical Gaze

'You cannot be free if you are contained within a fiction.'
—Julian Beck, *The Life of the Theatre*

Theory is a place of circumstantial reality
which doesn't actually exist. At its core
are questions about how we read others
and how we are read by them. We can all
misremember through multiple voices
and manifold perspectives, burrowing
into sweet, dark places of fecundity,
novels and paintings and architecture,
even poems, making them our own and
writing parasitic criticism before laying
little translucent eggs, pollinating novels
to make more novels, turning the breath
of the living into irrational knowledge.

The critical gaze is tearing us apart;
we learn to be by simply being, unfolding
our personae, mapping and re-mapping
the self onto others, onto art or literature.
Being taught in this way feels forbidden,
the remove makes it only sweeter but
it is another idea that helps the reader
understand what could be going on.
Ignore the aside in an earlier chapter,
the norms of chronology and narrative;
after all, parataxis, chance, fragmentation
are how many of us experience the world
and like our reading to reflect that. I haven't
read it all yet but as well as being obsessed
I don't pursue expected lines of thought.

Image and information overload lack depth
or meaning, are working differently, find

readers in the wreckage of biography, dread
and excitement. Both dystopia and utopia
signify nothing which has not happened yet;
everything changes when the world can only
be read by considering webs of associations,
connections, connotations, perpetual motion
occasionally broken up by over-zealous poets,
jagged editing and fractured time. Reviewers
suggest that reading is not working: people
are interested in moments, places and their
responses to and memories of them. There is
an absence throughout the book, missing
rather than fractured time. Improvisation
is a narrative shaped like itself by narrative
shaped itself by chance in the middle of
the moment. Everyone has just left this
mediated and constructed fiction, wandered
off to track down lost locations, looking for
obscure references, a perpetual state of mind.

There are many costume changes, sets can be
dismantled overnight; these experiences are
easier to talk about afterwards. In some ways,
you are manipulating reality, as you continue
to attempt to grasp something no one can
understand: fictional real life fiction breaking
the rules using different rules. It is unclear
if we will ever get truth bolted together, is
all about perspective, about the angle that
you're looking from as we fall into language.
If the actual mechanism is hard to discern
don't bother reading from beginning to end.
Discernment still facilitates the process of
interpretation, expression and communication,
allows readers to pretend they understand.

3. Sensation

I want things to only happen
when the world around me changes,

can sense I'm made of the same materials
as our planet, that we both need caring for

as well as thinking machines to document
the multiple dimensions between inner selves

and the outside world, create a highly original
and comprehensive overview of forms of body.

What are these types of energy that we sense?
How does the brain interpret the information

it receives? I have always been interested
in predictions, want things to only happen

when they occur. It gets more fascinating
and much weirder, is one thing to allow that

there might be an alternative perspective
on colour, but quite another to accept

that colour doesn't actually exist outside
our brains. What does it mean to be alive?

Processing incoming information is known
as perception, the brain actively collects

and organises data, regulates and conditions.
Signals from the outside world are interpreted

and layered with prior expectations and emotions.
This is the seat of all knowledge and personality,

the home of your innermost thoughts, the place
where you experience everything. Sensations

provide perceptual links to the world, allow us
to write the autobiography of each other's lives.

I can feel the morning breeze, taste aniseed,
sense the intuited evidence of invisible worlds.

4. Inevitable

'In a sense, it might be seen as inevitable that an artistic experiment
entirely devoted to the celebration of the here and now stubbornly
resists its own immortalization as a work of art.'
    —Tilman Baumgärtel, *Now and Forever*

You can't pretend accidents don't play their part.
In fact, the pivoting joints were organised using
calculations based on the exploitation of bounce
in relation to phenomenology and tape delay.

Writers take possession of accidents and errors
and stitch them together, suspend the presence
of the world for a brief moment, make it closer
to temporal rather than narrative experience.

You can't pretend faith doesn't play its part.
Transcendence lives in proximity to doubt
open within circles activated with a kind of
psychological awakening to their own being.

Perhaps the fierce wind that created everything
is God, perhaps it was a final attempt to obtain
perpetual motion using only gravity and inertia?
All the calculations were checked by an engineer

but you can't pretend chance won't play its part.
The stories we tell are why the number of words
is always growing as time to read is running out.
Everyone plays with repetition and difference,

consumes the now just as they do everything else.
In our world, things acquire meaning not through
their own individual properties but through the
remaining fragments of perception they become.

You can't pretend we know exactly what is what.
I am always surprised that this voice belongs
to me, wherever I find the words. Poetry is more
a name for process than a prospectus for belief.

Amlanjyoti Goswami

Pia Tafdrup's Book

At the exhibition, the slender poet
Waits by the desk, draped in elegant chiffon.

Her book is lying on a table of grainy wood.
I grab it, like a treasure, a rainbow of surprise.

It is about a piano, a simple tune
Dressed in notation, as if music.

I am so delighted I rush to tell
My academic friend about it, the one who knows it all.

I check the book on Google and Wikipedia
And it is the same one.

I check the price.
Way too expensive for me.

An out-of-print edition, from twenty-five years ago
But the cover is the same.

I've never seen the book before
And yet the exhibition is real, real as the poet standing next

To the book, with pictures being clicked.
I look for the poems online, wondering which one is true

The book – or – this feeling – slipping into water,
Swimming home, those dark lapland lights twinkling.

The language of water

Prahlad changes house pipes.
He knows the language of water, its changing colour
Where to make it stop, how to work a cistern.

Spirit levels bend to the hush of daylight
Waters gush, then spurt a feeling –
How water moves – or doesn't – early morning.

Nothing travels from the kitchen tap.
Here he is, fixing a swollen pipe
Rats on the floor, they've been there before

Gnawing everyday like a fresh storm
They know not when to stop.
This one's electrical, he says, finally

The pump burnt, too hot, too much sorrow.
Get a new one, or wire up the old one
In a way the waters won't know.

Flow. Teach water to stay still
But it won't listen.
One day you pull a lever in the middle of a fever

And there it gushes again, like new beginning, like language
Bursting at the seams.
Today will still be beautiful.

Valeria Melchioretto

The Shortest Day

sicut in caelo et in terra…

On winter's solstice Pegasus fell from the sky to die in our garden.
It must have slipped or knocked its head on Cassiopeia's vanity,
but while the Queen of Aethiopia had seized the North Star firmly
so she would not drop from her height, the poor horse stumbled.

Despite wings it fell to earth with countless snowflakes in its train.
Its once pure coat turned mourn black as it rushed through space,
then broke its neck on the spot where mother's roses are out of bloom.
There I find it in the morning; far from fame and glory, far from home.

Its body lies in the dirt, fragile and final. On its black back, slick and soft,
pearls of perspiration resemble a constellation. Can a myth ever die
or is death just a myth? A crowd gathers but there is no explanation
or consolation. Still, much is said while the snow slowly turns to slush.

What would mother make of such a stark omen if she were still alive?
I raise my head to see if Andromeda is still securely chained to her rock
and realise, that I am the rock to which my world is scarcely bound.

Orphaned by Default

Despite its years, my heart resents being orphaned.
It resembles a split pomegranate not meant for my chest.
Yet perhaps this is as inevitable as original sin and the fall
made me inherit father's plight and mother's sorrows
with so much sour cordial to stain the sky east and west.

The robins peck the red berries as if it could shorten winter
and parrots prize juicy seeds from the ventricle chambers
as if its taste could take them back to their exotic paradise,
magpies fancy them to be garnets or rubies of exquisite worth,
but the sweet orb is no longer related to joyous fruitfulness.

Plundered, till all that remains is a husk where red ink bled
into laments. It's the shell of a vital organ with papery walls
on which prayers are written with an unsteady hand, tremulous
as if frost had set in, verse hurts, words are dictated by birds
with the pattern known from songs that spring in the windpipe.

This strange fruit got into my ribcage the way Persephone
entered hell: fate put it there as a reminder that life is round
and all is dialectic, all is a digestion which we must obey.
Once taken food, even from strangers, destinies fuse and
they become familiar as we belong to them beyond the grave.

City of the Dead in the Kingdom Beyond the End

By day the city seems a manmade mountain, piercing the parish.
Built on three heavy tiers; earth bank, red rock and pure pity
each weighing God's name down and bending it deep until
it touches a raw nerve that chimes loud yet hollow in the bones.

No matter how much I aim to reach that hilltop it's always apart
as if it were a paradox walled off by fierce nettles under my skin.
The drumming in my throat as I ascend keeps my feet on the ground
and makes me cling to my appearance which ages, aches and recalls.

But by night the city comes alive like an imploded birthday-cake
for over a hundred brave centenarians, eternal flames for a battle
against darkness and frost. A touch of electricity not taken lightly,
suspended on a thin wire under glass triggers tender brainwaves.

The electric spark in those fake candles, more copious than stars,
is dull if I compare it with that glint in your eyes when you jested.
No whimpering, wailing or weeping brings back your warm glow
as your image twitches and itches inside my skull like an amputation.

Tending a Garden in Despair

For you I plant purple petunias as there is no more use for greens.
Last year's carrots were stifled in growth by sticky red clay.
Snails riddled the cabbages, weeds made the beans below par.

The courgettes had only brought forth big yellow trumpets;
so silent, so sickly, so sobering, so sly but no fruit followed.
Begonias are now as good a remedy as pills and doctor's orders.

The pomegranate tree grows on the edge between worlds.
What effort to hose that arid soil where jasmine pleases bees.
But no matter how much water I carry to the end of the night,

when the wood pigeon calls thrice, the earth is as eager as you.
As darkness falls into your throat you want to leave without shoes.
I cannot hold on to your breath, sage blooms yet life turns blind.

The sunflowers are taller than the shallots could have been but also
give me cause for tears as my childhood thirsts for your voice.
Now my shadow comes out every evening to paint the roses black.

Finn Haunch

Engine Confessional

Their knees couched in gelatine pads, three workmen clustered
to a box junction. They could be the famed luminaries
from the council, which we wait to see all our lives –
maintainers of the power grid.
They could've been said to be praying
at this unsociable hour,
stooped awkwardly under a pylon
with looped-wire rosaries in-hand, voltmeter as *spiritus mechanicus* –
but downwind of the devotionals,
there are so many broken souls shuffling out of the nightshift
by the petrol station, all disappearing into a bus depot
where the dodgy, silent kids smoke dope at the door.

And this one woman in a handstitched shawl, a nurse's uniform,
she blows a fiver she can't afford
on a bunch of sellotaped, cellophaned flowers.
Winds' getting up again –
the last of the leaves are loosening up
like a badly built wardrobe. The lads are chewing
on biros, something is ticked off
and pondered over. Tab-ends burn up, become little lives.

Weeks earlier, there was an incident up there.
Things were organised online. There was a decent turnout
with posters and placards,
protest and a counter-protest,
though no-one official. They made a sort of wayside shrine
from a signal box
beside the roundabout,
the thin rusted doors
hinged open to a weak, washed-out sun –

flowers, fosters, toon scarfs,
and under them the
mouldy diodes clumped together
and slung up over a grid of soldered-on hooks,
barely blinking, the damp split rubber
and wet gaps stuffed with torn-up
metro tickets, which go nowhere in particular.

Our Meera's come back this morning, clutching flowers
at 5 a.m., only to find the workmen here
in their vestments of high-viz.
Their heads are pressed into the paving stones, necks craned
into a dripping, fungal darkness
to find a fault none of us would know to look for.

There was nothing to be done
but take up the last, waterlogged, laminated picture of her dead boy
from the hard shoulder.

Fiona Larkin

The Unthank

Once, I received gifts
I could not reciprocate.

I kept them anyway.
Sometimes a no is hard to take.

Words twitch on the tongue, not
the honey you remember

but the sweetish rot
of something on the turn

bitten back at sore expense.

Fugue

I play you to my inner ear
where the canal's on fire:
a musical malfunction?
Restless beneath my feet,
earth threatens to release
my staggered self.

Like tinnitus you're echoing,
insisting that I listen,
clicking mandibles
clattering a tune,
something in the timbre
unknown, remembered.

Blame it on my openness:
this unplugged aperture,
a readiness to hear again
the counterpoint you sing,
your entirely intoxicating
and possibly viral air.

Lethal

immersed at last
in the river's spate

a pebbled rush
a dash that deafens

earth's residue
a stain to bleach –

he's a yellowed leaf
all helplessness

where ripening's lost
fruit forgotten

as if the flow
rots memory

turns frog to tadpole
back to spawn

who cares – not he
now bud now seed

rinsed clean of all
that made him sing

Peter Dukes

Three Lagrangians

I
Paradiso rough—copy dot   dispensed imped
factive the swallows repelled, late shortfalls
            in March—the snows ringing the out-post
rippling chlorosis out of the whirlwind   shall
the plummets of heaven its jars and funnels
            rain through in heels and pleats loosed   like
stays and splines the line upon it thick darkness,
            sunk roads, uncomely healed—   Ungiven,
when they couched in dens or shuttered from verges
slowing in an evening's ochre   I felt my
            mind damned freighted   arch   rhododendrons'
            the jostle   hope fast apex meri–
            stems flaming into the air or reaped
of night, left in earth and warmed from dust—rip forth

                Mazzaroth   in his seasons

II
By the willows of the brook   a deep shore copped
silken rage wind-hardened   terracotta veils
            dis-possession—the crumbs turning
            in air, the tidal mound covered from
folds, worked loose in right shaking jolt surrenders—
Nolde looking both ways neither happier
            nor sodden clef its thunder drawing
up Jordan to his mouth afront ache votive
sorbus anthem foul

                        tempo   aryl knock joint
            crape amongst the dewy trees, and—

flint gravel exhilarant   cordial   thought
      rapt apparel the dead when last
dumb lily obedient   Sedge forced left
below advent bittering—bell match ardent

          tongue, parry its cord drawn down

III

A belt or cloud sent toppling through the merry
      larks more iron than carbon water
phaeton turning in its sunlit dust hearts'
attuned in a thorny wood squalling beauty
stroke fore damnation—fire-myth died Ate false
      but she made mouths, from horizon
slippered—spring fields candour sufferance gripped
wind-lashed little blunt mouse-ear repulse—and with
      a back and with a front lax basal
rubble terra cleft

          riddled clap teasel burned

jade vantage—for his hands that claw and rigid
      fail

        as piece of the nether mill-stone
      sharp under, sewn in windfall—greet
fanning ark ever strikes charm anoint the un–

         seen shelf curt zigzag clover

D'or Seifer

Autotomy

Once I believed in you
a homeland
living simply
with no hurt.

But how can you love with no memory
the world reborn at the end of the journey
leaving only recipes
tattered flavours from *The Pale*
stories about woodcutters and bears
not neighbours nor childhood friends.
Life the only belonging you carried.

Discarding the tongue you were born with
like a lizard discards its tail
adopting an ancient one
regrown.
Painting poetry
in a placeless language —
that is art's line, growing grapefruits,
squeeze-turning until art takes new form.

Half a helix
a spiral blowing in the wind.
I do not carry you in photos but
in texts inscribed upon my memory,
as if *written in pencil in the sealed railway car.*
Fear of abandoned bags,
a partial story passed on.

I have sung the old songs
and now unlearn their tropes.

I am a writer of new texts
 an air-plant
carried on the wind.

I live in a jar with no soil.

Vowsounds/Kol Nidrei

When I was four
my grandmother took me to *shul*
on the day of atonement
and in the quietest moment
after the call and response,
when only the cantor recites,
I loudly inquired –
"Savta, do you believe in God?"
she whispered "Shhhh. Later."

My name was still written in the book of life that year.

I was a witness to belief
held in silence
truth parting.

Do you believe in transmutation?

I do.
I have felt the transformations.
Lead rubs paper
the blunted pencil's pressure, every letter a consecration
a squid's fear flowing through pen
an oath
proscribed on pages of blue lines.

Fingers tap symbols: firing neurons transferred into light on a screen.

What is transformed?
What burns, passes through membranes, down axon terminals?
What transpires in the Holy of Holies, where only the High Priest can enter?

Where consecrations turn to silent sound,
voices turn your voice into my own,
credo beyond emotion, past music.

When poets use timeless tools
when my lips don't move
but I feel something
moving, when words
turn into heartbeats, echo through chambers
when the spaces between words are systoles.

I believe in text
timeless like prayer

that I might blow and shape these words,
no longer mine
beyond form and lines
material and symbols
beyond metaphor.

Sometimes when I read your words I know
beyond faith:
I have read a vow that cannot be unspoken –

> *Our words their space and taste*
> *their sounds and shapes are shared.*

Words turned white
alive
eternal.

Mark Byers

Polychoral (notation 1)

step beneath a canopy   of birdsong
             its nuthatch/
coloratura   or simply the common
sluicing of the river   against

exposed beech roots   alder wands
    man-made banks/
denser rhizomes   unco-
       ordinated sounds
I say *simply* –   turning along
       my habitual path/
where the calls   limn
horsechestnuts and retreating

               blackberries/
agile impromptus over
      microtones//frayed edges
cantor / cantrix /
         sing to the choir

Fieldwork

on a new path you look   //plainly without
         the clutter of names //
their counterfeit and dull//   alloy
leaning towards   //littoral
   meanings/   signifying on an edge

      a mycorrhizal singsong
           between
distant oaks//   or the lichen's call

    and response//   its holding
patterns   branched, candelabraed
     or leaf-like//   lessons in *politic*

seeing barely//   at the interstice
     indecipherable signals
their ungovernable//   idiom

driving the A695 east from Hexham (notation 3)

indistinctly: a kestrel
      crowds the dry-
          stone wall,
      moss-sleeved //
        and white lichen
its spots and streaks
            on downy buff
and black remex
hellbent on shrew
         or vole// un-
knowing machine
           behind its haft
of beak// and variegated
         plumage, I
      catch you against a
lattice of iron-gray //
      slate and fieldstone
    courting mouse
        and metaphor

&

on one of the days we went to see
her because she was dying my
grandmother pointed under the
desk & screamed there were devils
& then she looked up at the
bathroom's darkness & shook
with maybe withdrawal but it
seemed like death & all the time
she lay there wrapped in too-white
sheets that stank of terror and
bleach & then she took my hand
& I felt her heart beating through
her fingers like a train coming off
tracks over long grasses & she had
almost no teeth but she said quite
clearly so I still hear it *please please
kill me* & my sister said something
with her breath that sounded like
prayer & we were all very quiet &
the still of the room was terrible
& then she went to sleep but her
eyes kept moving behind her lids
& she didn't die for several years
& when she did of course I wasn't
there

We Came Home

to find a madman in the living room
sucking his teeth. He kicked the coal bronze,
the carved song from my father.
I'll go for a reawakening, I told him.
He sensed my disbelief, reached for it.

Outside, comfort shook itself from the upstairs
window & a shower of breath disturbed
the pond like catastrophe. Your host
of death hawkers swept in to dance
over water as pain weaponised, pure heat.

The rest of the garden junk:
    a single, discarded disloyalty
    an empty bottle of seers
    a love life in need of re-fitting
    waste

I opened my book of pretence.
He signed his name, said *It's not lust, it's art.*
You came downstairs
holding a hammer,
licked the pen from the page.

Dominic Fisher

Earth mass

Then we go down broken, in a thick sleep, into the elements
that make us and also make that black bread underneath us
which takes the living to itself, feeds on our bone and sinew
stem and feather, flesh and shells, the nitrogen, the calcium.
We'll add in our small measure of blood or ash, and become
uncountable among grains of soil as they're sifting falling sea
and as winters lock then unlock damp stumps, teeth of mice
and crumbs of trees in the grub and slow-worm underworlds.
How did we think we could ever hold it with our promises
the ground and bread we've broken all this time and wasted,
and is it time we were re-absorbed, perhaps to be returned,
as leaves maybe, some nameless month early in the season?
Moons, worms, the tilting of the world would work the earth
very well without us while we're going disjointed round again.

Dog fox barking

After Vasko Popa

You bark

that your juniors should give way
steer clear of these overgrown lanes
and leave the scent clean

You bark

that cats should know who's coming through
get off their high fences
and fuck off indoors

You bark bark

that walls and sheds should echo you
and stop us in our well-lit kitchens
that territory we built mazes on
for tonight is returned to you

You bark bark bark

that your blood relatives should hear you
in the damp black and your half-brother
your rival should bark bark back

Marie-Louise Eyres

A Well-Tuned Eye

If it could, this eye
would release a slow whine,
in B flat, as an accordion might.

Each plaintive cry
begs a cool compress
padded with lavender.

Long term, I'm offered
a scorching laser-beam
and a sweaty, rubber mask.

Flashes arrive on the left,
out of nowhere
like portals opening

into an animated universe
where everything
shimmers in silver.

Oh, sing me some god-damned
Brahms why don't you,
while I rest my head

on soft flannel sheets
in the dark.

Symbiosis

As this casket made of willow-grass rots down,
cold flesh, all blood gone dark,
shall blend with earth's brown gypsum,
red hematite.

Reaching under-forests,
those sprawling, fungal threads,
I'll join colonies of lion's mane,
pale-skinned milk-tooth,
fast growing finger paths of light
amongst black trumpets.

And buried deep,
past hungry worms, I'll mimic
spore-like symbiosis at tips
of Jacarandas across the California hills,
offer nitrogen in fair exchange
for sugar from tree root.

Then I may just bear witness
to each subsequent spring bloom,
the bee dances,
swift, ruby-throated hummingbirds
on the dip, monarch butterflies
stringing the heights of twisty,
purple ferns.

Courtesy of mushroom,
life shifts mycologically
from cell to tube to petal.
In the shade of indigo trees,
violet has mixed
with curd white bone.

John Greening

Oracles

Tells you only what you know,
Know, but dare not realise.
—Lawrence Durrell, 'Delphi'

For you
       Mrs Simmons
                is still
declaiming
          one of the tragedies

         *

I approach
          the oracle

         *

My first question
                What is the point
My second
          Why does nobody know
and others
          fit for a leadership debate
or an English lesson
               the kind I dream

         *

Oh and
       why last night
were we
       so vividly

debt collectors
                in a tenement
demanding cash
                 and who was that
annoyed not to be recognised
I just served you your meal

*

Oracles
        cries Mr Hill

*

Having finished Divination
by Signs and Inspired Divination
in Flaceliere's little book

I was starting on the Oracle
at Delphi but broke off to look

for ways to make room on my shelves

trying to find the smallest crack
in the slim volumes for a fat Collected

*

Taking one I hadn't noticed,
and never read
                a hardback
black dusty unappealing
dated *mcmlxvi*
to give to charity
                  opening
the book at once I saw the title
Delphi

*

Let us go back
to the beginning
like that ballad
over the credits of our favourite
Scandi Noir
clearly English
but impenetrable
and visit
Heathrow
the Druid temple
beneath Runway One
If I stood
holding up an old-fashioned
white paddle
would I behold
the future
taking off into
the distance or distances I've flown

*

Or better
revisit Luxor
walk the enclosure of Amun-Re
at Karnak
those astonishing
huge pillars we press our hands to
not knowing what will happen
only that they will all be dead
at some point

*

as now they are
all
or almost all
my father
did not need the help of Norns
the raven was always on his shoulder

44

your mother
        spilt
                without the Sibyl's
earthless guidance

          *

            but you go on
translating the *Odyssey*
across the flowery meadow of
our dining room table
the cat spread out in all his
laziness as far as **μ**

Maria Jastrzębska

When I was your age

the dead watched
      with eyes open all hours

and the flat stare of security
      cameras in corners

Did they spy on us
      making love?

If we whispered
      could they hear?

We heard them even
      as they fell silent

a rustle like wind that picks up
      dry husks of wasps

at the end of summer
      only to drop them again

When we saw a programme
      about young seals

their mottled bodies
      washed up headless

on sand and rock, the dead cried
      Look! They're just like us!

turning our attention back to themselves
      as usual

When I was your age

horses trembled after charging
their great bodies unable to
stop shaking The street in front
of them reared up people
shouting no screaming Placards
cracked banner poles cans
rolled under their hooves
everyone running hard pushing
to squeeze together onto the
pavement as glass shattered
More screams mirrored their
fear Tails swishing fast the
horses threw back their heads
jumping sideways kicked out
despite their training looking for
a way out like us as their riders
tried to calm them We held onto
one another flattened against
shop windows pleading for
air then the riders turned the
horses round to charge back up

Peter Larkin

Blockwoods Weren't Unknotting This (extract)

as if to unlock blockade
or release it to its interferences,
on the way of, across the path of

at a staple arable of trees
the stamped root of assistance
is occupational

resistance at its sprung palliatives   vertical risk goes cagey over its fir
extensives

amend a tree to its structural tabs, cramp it co-attended   tokens of
latitude, remitting   chastened amplitudes

evenly blockage will 'skim' across any other alleviate package, prowling
kernel at a shawling scrape of access/recess

is the prevention: anticipates in block formation its ontological spurt
(weight)   the sweep tarries until its own graining will have reached an
across   to flow with each encapsulated stub

a reversion concession recodes (coats) the circling horizontals, is hood
and cloak to a contrary compression, not one fleck looser

an ob-struct vents the green cascade   immediate rim rehearses a seating
it immersed, thickly occurs across stripped

a leaner channel taps
its own vestiges, festoons
the pressure lock, stoppages
unblanked

how a runnel cribs its shoring   its through-to implants abreast   punches
(graces) butts of crustfilm, trimflow, groundflood

as the slippage is clipped with this, fetched at the sudden shutdown
onset of sharp symbolic wastage, its spread (vantage) terrain   without
which the secreted horizontals starve

constriction at the plunge itself bulges unknown envelope   unflowns
rake up and seal plenties by vertical relation   diagonal breadth of the
post-open, preliminary meta-release

ample tumble trails the knot, on the exact   a basketed spire whose pull
encumbers each living wire   offskirted for a knot's inner fringe

moored bulge not hulk grants body   its ropes at a covering of unpaused
germ   a range ahead of a lunge disdains the fresh flesh, re-cairns the
crash of it   the crush of its bulk becoming, becalming

banked / swarmed / harmed at the resting ferment   now a little
intimate with post-torment   the interlocking rudder is vertical
shudder   each surface shrinks (shivers) the contingents of another

> climax plane at its embrace
> again, vertical at depthless
> relief bordering: fords
> horizon knot for knot

acclimatised reserve, the binding only bold for lightest tendril   edge
rivets (enspirited) don't themselves alight   re: the co-blight of

what not yet let go set from margin towards sore ventral offer   on
behalf of a not yet shared non-release   knots will spot the entrance, not
increase   tether (allow span for) some membrane of reception

tie the sills, it instirs within ante-lapse, proto-pulse   at the back of any
pre-looped standing knots are binary remit, hailing delay for its one other
course   diversion unadorned, poorly (faithfully) sheered at the touch

a tree's congestion hurtles
its shrubbing, requites unstealthy
verticals   truly nondescript once
unbroken in common choir

tender ruin qualifies for prediction, slenderness reassessed the rim   no
neuter is as chancing as steeps of this   spared horizontal at knotted
creep   scarce not rampant, collates the stickiness of behalves on
betweens

veins taller for lashes, spears of attachment, knots of fruition   befell
the provenience of implicity, total transfer *at* its clotting

loose, unslashed traps in
relay-trips   real otherness
which included them
around our own blockages,
green baggage

not trivial preventive, blocking
is deformable but embedded:
an unknot stuck at/is
its particular traverse
across the grain

a tangle diagram so blocked out as to label its leaf for airy minimal touch
    attachment by holding the miracle to its least

freedom continuous arc
tasking-over the crossing,
garment-fold group of a knot
its overheads relieve (relive)
block for block

the error of meaning it tree-prominent   duration of block averaging
already salvaging repletion at its blunter less possible, actual to a least

float block from blockade along a pacing-large arena   the quota is
natural wood distilled by each truss of the grain

        the replication block only
        solid at a leaf's horizon,
        lone freefall to a treeful
        of the unknot

Aaron Lopatin

Will one plow there with oxen?

And what, I wonder, did the rabbi
say about mistake.

The way it galls and shackles
and architectures on your soul:

        The abandoned abacus strains.

        Rain water fills a bucket to the brim.

        Horses worry that we never live again.

        We mistake the taste of hemlock for the truth.

The Room / The Field / The Sanctuary (Daiyenu)

The offerings avoidance of; the smell
            of burnt potato; play a trumpet

for a mouse; take my feet off
            at the door; enough of it to build

a whole; slash the screen door;
            crack the attic; enough of it to dig

genizahs; burrow in the fields;
            to harpy; heap in ranges; patch

and dapple in the light (amen); enough
                              of it to split the pits out from the

fruits; to bring us home; to dry the land;
                              would it be sufficient?

Coronas

Walls, water, stores
of bones:

a beaver builds a dam:
a bower birds a bower:

by the hour
bodies drop

while people pray,
unending, in their

maudlin: this
a, sort of, rising

of the lights?

David Dumouriez

Morning at Galata

It's not the waking. More the how, or why.
The younger me would think, at those
abysmal hours, that all the beautiful
would be asleep and just the average
or the desperate ones were up. I'd take
the bus and look at the imperfect, the
dishevelled, as we passed them,
stop-by-stop. I'd see the onion eyes
of those who entered; watch them
lurching down the aisle towards a seat.
The beautiful must be asleep, I'd think.
They must. They should!

But another beauty never slept.
Perhaps I didn't care to see it. Was
committed to resist. Ultimately, maybe,
something switched. I saw the city first.
The place. The space we borrow from the cats.
I learned, perhaps, what people meant
who said they volunteered to track
the sun's ascent. To the right, I viewed
the city half in gold, and further out
the greying panoramic channels issuing
an open invitation: "Look, I've made it easy
for you – come and be another Canaletto!"
And there, off to the left, around
the domes, I nodded as I saw those
spears that try to touch the spirits,
but fall within the human range.
This place and its transitions: the
parts that break into another age,

then break again. But stay. A city
living, always, on the edge of
natural demolition (as so, repeatedly,
we're told!). Just trust the cats.
The cats will tell us when.

I see it better now. This place.
A place with few superiors to visit?
Check.
A place requiring fortitude to stay?
I've paid my toll.
A place in which to live and wish
to think is often to despair? *(Too true,*
according to the ones who know.)
But 'good' can swallow 'bad'.
And states and angles change.

Mark Goodwin

Through A Crystal of Daylight
In A Field Overlooking A
Llŷn Peninsula, A September 2022

The idea of a crystal alone
floating in the void without a
background to reflect, is a fiction.
  —Douglas S. Duckworth, *Tibetan Buddhist Philosophy of Mind and*
  Nature (drawing from Sūtra Explaining the Intent)

We imagine with our bodies and in place,
never without the ingredience
and the co-operation of both.
  —Edward S. Casey, from his preface to the second edition of *Imagining*

                    as gem

-sheer sun
light cements

                        drystone walls as

glints through gaps
blacken blocks as

            wind squeaks grasses' edges as

gorse glows its golds a
gainst sky's one wide blue

                              thought as

black flakes of choughs
divine un

        seen curls of air so

a young
chestnut stallion now

              releases

his silvery fl

    ag of piss &

      scent of apples (his

alcohols of
autumn windfall) this

           alive icon
           empty

    ing noth
    ing

Wheatear Gathers, A May 2022

in memory of my Dad

the place, the gathering power, gathers in and preserves all it has gathered, not like an encapsulating shell, but rather by penetrating with its light all it has gathered, and only thus releasing it into its own nature. —Martin Heidegger

Swinside Stone
Circle's tall

est spike of
ground a

        cob of mineral grains

has at its
point a

    small moor
    bird of

slate-blue
-grey that's

black/white
flashed and

dawn-o

range chested
his eye-

st
ripe's black

hold
ing his

          glint

ing bead of
seeing

Neal Hoskins

Note from the Villa Arcetri, 1638

A sky of voices above a land bright from rain. Heat humming in the tree light with murderous glare. Firenze's drumming pageant rumbles on with the passing storm. The cicadas swell his mind. Their sound is a wall of black mist along a line of cypress trees, etching in the shadows, inking him to the landscape. He sees hooded men with knives, he sees a window, and arriving with the dark, there is a voice – Il Signor Milton è arrivato.* There, Galileo finally. Hovering. His face painful, absorbed. Like someone feeling for the darkness. In his pocket, a letter's seal melts like a wound; it bleeds with dark words spinning an underworld. Note the tremendous scrawl of Italian ink. Tear to the line: *Every time I wake up, I go blind again.*

Mr Milton has arrived

Prelude to Rain, 1940

where the dark of a window
on a train becomes a line of soldiers
on horses and a river in the rain
there in the forest by the fire
they will sing down a carriage
where pianos play and they believe
they will be home and safe again
a broken monastery appears
in the windows of the train
oxygen of letters written back
in the rain moves through the sky
on a soldier's face of pain
something about the poetry of us
was left standing in the rain

Track, 2023

People said he took a dog for a child that was gone. When there was a sound from the room the dog walked in with heavy eyes just from sleep. They went to hotels and walked by railway lines. Sometimes it rained and the dog had damp fur with a rich smell. Cities suited them; they met people in town squares, the dog liked the dark trees and watched the lines of silver horses breathing under them. When they went back to the room to eat and watch late-night tv the man would sit and talk to the dog for a time, and they would look out of the window at the railway tracks. The dog listened to him and searched for something in his eyes and arms, then he slept by the side of the bed while the man continued to speak to the window. The man thought about how dogs found each other, how they barked miles off before coming into view. The man stood over the sleeping dog in the orange lamplight and turned to watch the passing trains stream by his view. When it rained again the man told the dog the child was gone. He watched the sleeping dog closely and listened to his presence in the room.

Amber Rollinson

Birdwatchers

When my first sighting becomes
our first sighting, I think –
of island through mist, towering cliffs
the turquoise wrinkle of frantic Atlantic
think – the cliffs are grey-blue, like bruises
swelling through grassy sideland skin
You think you are afraid of deep water, and boats
but cross to look as puffins fly –
as seabirds gather, and people gather
to see their busy swoop and dive –
You think this footpath is the one to the cove
find steps which crumble into unsolved
conversations among land and edgeland and sea
Here is battery wall, here is grass like sponge
here is birdwatcher searching for something
dropped as we cross ledge together, reach sharper edge
Afraid of heights, you stare down, look –
at strange little men in smart tuxedos
heaps of sand eels caught in tiny teeth
as they feed we feed on seasickness tablets
think of explaining bird and its habits
with only the words for you and me

Behind the Door, Another

after Dorothea Tanning

you might say I lead a double life, triple, multiple, manifold
painting pulverised wrenched from place to place, gnawing
my way into another's eyes, visitor, worrier, unwelcome guest
but stay and I will stay a while. Open the door, now walk
corridors in gloom, the moon takes a velvet bite of night
it's feeding time for bats and foxes, sharks and painters who
rest on their bellies, hunt in the half-hearing out of focus
this vertigo of deep subconscious, who closes the door too late

When no one is watching

when no one is watching
the greatest pleasure
triangle of sunlight on wall
so perfect, crisp-edged, warm
above sharp-eyed tail-flicker
magpie or some hidden
traveller from another place
here today, gone tomorrow
fresh as the day that passes
when no one watches I double
dip or do my best work or listen
without moving to the whirring
wind, stirs the heart of things
when no one is watching
the magpie comes in, talks

John Phillips

This Isn't a Painting

As a painter tries to find the simplest form in order to discard all painterly effects, making the one thing capable of being seen the idea he had to express, the poet must work to make sure the poem isn't noticed, that it's as invisible as possible.

Braque: His Final Palette
for Alex Danchev

raw umber
                burnt umber
raw sienna
                burnt sienna
yellow ochre
                orange-yellow
                Naples yellow
ultramarine
                lamp black
                vine black
                bone black

Conversation with Miroslav Holub

Some say they are poets
because they write poems
some say they're poets
only when writing poems

(not before/not after)
some say a poet is
when others say so
some say why pay attention
to whoever calls themselves a poet
some say everyone's a poet whether they write or not
some don't mention poets or poems

Apologia
for Graham Jelbert

Remembering the dead's not easy
Even their dreams have gone
Don't think for a moment they remember us
Or care one way or another

Answer
for John Levy

Poems
can be multiplied
to mean more than they do alone

but if divided
they become less than silence

which is more than nothing is

or does

which equals what?

Nic Stringer

Poems from
even the stones the builder rejected [Foundations]

[Fiction]

Like the truth I am unfamiliar and distant, and not to be found half way between two propositions, or hiding behind bark with the sugar gliders, patiently waiting for beetles and flies. This does not make me irrational or extreme – being in the middle won't get you closer to reality, or to home. The middle is a slight thing, you must sit with your hand raised. It will lock you in.

Like the truth I am not at peace. I am a shapeshifter, mythic monster
          a bird you'd normally regard as unclean even in flight
  contact   and take off
        contact   take off   like the truth
    like a magician   carrier
narrative machine

[Fabric]

Pure grained and almost translucent, it's a kind of parlour trick. A man lying dead, veins raised and still pulsating on the forehead, a veil carved from the same crystalline limestone, scatters light. There is no obvious cause of misery, no lengthening of fingers from hands too fragile to hold the weight of a sagging body, or fluid filling the chest

but a veil, where a veil should not be possible. A very particular aspect of this death.

[Fissure]

I don't see the big picture only scattered objects that can be identified individually. This is like standing in a field watching sheep, one sheep at a time and not knowing there is this thing called 'flock.'

I recognise the form, then can't make sense of its place. It's the same with gadgets and body parts. I understand what a 'finger' is, or 'wrist,' 'knuckle,' 'nail.' But what's to be made of 'hand'? Give me directions I will remember a tree, as a place of worship, just don't ask me to point to where I am on the map. This lack, of realisation, has caused me to lose a certain eagerness to smile. And when I smile, I am reborn   in the silenced response.

[Factions]

I am afraid of priests and clerics but a Televangelist is always pretty funny. It's better to separate the ghosts from strangers who look like us, you can usually tell the difference, only sometimes they are the same thing. We call them strangers but it's a trick of memory. I am a stranger myself. I don't know the full story, how other people tell the story, or where the library is – people craving a worthy life are only willing to take risks of nominal consequence

>   *open it up, take out the shell fragments, desiring danger*
>   *is a trick of memory too – a dog barking at strangers will*
>   *be subdued if you cover its head with a coat*

I used to believe with my whole soul what strangers told me. I wore their hair-lined gloves. They laughed without looking at me, without really surveying the damage, knowing I was afraid of their ordinariness

>   *there was a long silence before I could go back*
>   *for the dog and lose the gloves*

Half of me wants to stay where I am rooted, the other half would leave the dirt behind. Here, amongst the clouds and peaches I sweeten but see the storm coming.

[Fidelity]

I am chasing a flaming pearl to Heaven
an apparition that is not worthy of belief
but not contrary to the Faith either.

> The demigods of the moat and the walls
> are appalled by this ending of beauty
> the rain-bringing clouds and cycles of rifting
> boundary of tapestry weave silk
> exposed to the burning rays of the sun
> running to nothing

> sun disc rises with vermillion bird
> vermillion bird soars over waves
> waves combine with sky.

It takes more than a human effort
to read a dragon robe in Temple market.

Judi Sutherland

Fire Season

'It doesn't take much in the way of mind and body to be a lookout. It's mostly soul.' —Norman Mclean, 'A River Runs Through It'.

We can smell the burning gorse eight miles away
it billows into dirty cloud, yellowing the air
as tobacco stains a ceiling. Now, every continent
has Fire Season. I think of those writers

who like to work as 'lookouts' in National Parks
firewatching the forest for twelve bucks an hour
in order to have time to think, and write
the wilderness from the tops of wooden towers.

I've realised too late that I am a nature poet;
it's impossible to speak of landscape now
without the feeling you are crafting elegies.
If the Inuit have fifty words for snow,

I need a lexicon of flames. How many species are there?
How hot do they burn? What are their names?

May Morning at Ditchling Beacon

Coming up the hill through early grey
into the hush of the morning.
Standing, shivering, waiting, checking
which way is East, wondering
if this orange haze is just the lights of Lewes
below the horizon. The sky scrubbed
of clouds, the sheep, woolly huddles on the Downs.

When the sun rose, it was just a glow
then an edge then a rolling arc
then the afterburner of a rocket launch
while mist shifted in the hollows
like a turning tide. Summer was a cobweb
caught between the hedgerows
and their shadows, and out across the Weald
the birds bustled into song, and we sang too
Sumer is i-cumin in— Lhude sing, cuccu!
pouring a libation of mead on the altar
of the trig point. And it was hot, that summer.

Who was it said, that if the sun only rose
once a year, we'd all be there to see it?
I'm telling you this, so although you weren't there
watch with me now, watch the sky
burnish up to blue. And when we've gone
that dawn will still exist, the sunrise
and the singers, because that's what poems do.

The Roman Houses

At Binchester, so the story goes,
where the great legions once deployed
before their tours of duty at the Wall,

the houses of the Vicus remained occupied
until 1728. No doubt they were cold
and damp, and left lots to be desired

but that was also true of newer houses.
 Life, and architecture, remained unchanged
for the working people of Vinovia.

And the troops withdrew, and Rome was sacked,
Empires rose and fell, played out
their board games on the battlegrounds of Europe,

while in Binchester the roads grassed over,
stable blocks collapsed, the amphitheatre
filled with blown loam and weeds, and was

forgotten. But the humble houses,
if you maintained the roof, and paid
attention to the drains, were good

for fifteen hundred years, until those who lived there
neither understood how old they were
nor wondered who had built them.

The Heart as a Peach Stone

Because Latin is a tight-closed book to the
unschooled boy, Leonardo learns the world

　　with silverpoint, gum Arabic, oak
gall; recording all things mirrored in his
strong left hand.

　　Recto, the plunge of a battle-horse;
verso the angle subtended by a planet's
orbit.

　　When you are not taught what is
important, the face of St Anne and a
blackberry blossom carry equal weight.

　　It is, all of it, *Sapienza*. The flexion
and extension in the body of a cat; the
Arno, charted; the muscled map of a male
nude; each noted in the classroom of his
mind.

　　Here, the heart is compared to a
seed; a little peach stone germinates; the
great vessels rooted in the bowel,

　　or branching up, to flower behind
the eyes.

Natalie Shaw

Breaking into the Icehouse

The icehouse was locked I
didn't have a key, I
had only my hands, also I
knew there would be thick layers I
█████████████ before I
could perform *the rescue operation*. I
got through the outermost parts ok; I
had some light bleeding but not too bad, I
then reached an inner section ████████, I
nonetheless kept on undeterred, I
did it, I
hurt my hands in fact I
needed better tools, I
was performing *a rescue operation*. I
kept on, into the icehouse, I
bashed through the ghosts, I
hit their empty faces; I
smacked them, I smacked them, I
was performing ████████████. I
got through because I
had no other options but I

Life-Changing Chicken

מַה טֹּבוּ אֹהָלֶיךָ, יַעֲקֹב; מִשְׁכְּנֹתֶיךָ, יִשְׂרָאֵל

How lovely are your dwelling tents, O Jacob,
I go past them on my way to work:
BEER WINGS ANARCHY
Say the signs and I hanker for a bit of anarchy too.

I ate of the life-changing chicken and it was good –
My shame fell from me like the skin of a snake
It lay grey and lifeless on the pavement
And I did step over it

Unto the best parts, where everything was crispy
And tasted just right. My heart cried out
Oh, just so as I tore up
My payslip and sent it, now manna, g*dwards.

Wendy Allen

South of the Boating Lake, Unnoticed

After Barbara Hepworth's 'Single Form' 1961–62

I watch her side view, a thin, arched ridge, marking the
way she will move. Except forward is a fence and the
other side a lake. The making and the marking is made
difficult by the ledge she stands on, remaining straight
backed, she looks at him, at the lake, the danger of the
fence, the tight net of the green metal confines, notices
the plaque with her name on covered in concrete.

All the Ways

I'm not allowed to use fingers, or tongue, only rub
against you using the edge of breath. You leave
abstract gasps on the roped off surface of *All the
Ways I Want to Fuck You*. The artwork is carved from
marble. Its several layers hide the way you'll never
know if it's you I'm writing about. I wonder if you
taste the way I imagine – your tip laps sea, is library
still. You are salt quiet while I kiss the rim of you,
repeating slow over. There are arched sounds now in
the nub of it all.

Encryption

After Barbara Hepworth's 'Torso II (Torcello)', 1958

I take photographs of the marks on *Torso II*, wonder
would the number of times you've gone down on me
fit on this sculpture. There have been too many. I ask
if you are in love with me, watch the words depart
the garden via a patina tight cable. The message
sounds flat, you don't respond, so I ask instead what
colour the cup is you drink coffee from. You say blue
grey, I say limescale.

Robert Sheppard

from Poems of National Independence: liberties with Wordsworth's sonnets

Fair Star of evening, Splendour of the west

Big Bong at eleven, resonant in the North, voice
of my country, strong across swart horizon, above
White Cliff's Union Jack screen, carries like Big Bo
stooping over Britannia's spangled party bosom,
on the government's news feed; Bo's little bong
on the Number Ten gong (the Cum's boohooing!)
conspicuous to all nations – but not on the BBC.
This bong is my country's new anthem! Winking,
laughing, Bo waves his bombastic banners over
his fresh duties, puzzled, declares, *There, this*
dark spot is Global Britain's sphere. Sport thrives
under Go's new National Thrust. Bought spent men
linger with contempt, do not love her, my fingered
Kentish maiden flattened against freezing winter metal.

Is it a reed that's shaken by the wind

Regard the dogging camps flooded by Storm Bo,
my lords, liars, statesmen. We use face
recognition to *detect* the viral sick, *detain*
the feral poor, *deport* the febrile black! Bend
the law; lengthen sentences: legislate in haste!
These are the first fruits of office, unseemly
reverence to Bo's shuffling power. Brush
off the squirts with low yielding arts degrees.
Level up the local level crossings. Plough HS2
through the nookie-moist nooks of English ground.
Build bridges between our crumbling colonies. Tilt
the level playing field of Euro-trade in gems.
'Shame on you!' they cry as Priti leaves the
chamber, shaken by her stormy rush of wind.

Festivals have I seen that were not names

It's Bonaparty Bo's birthday party –
every day! Swaying on Carrie's motorbike,
he's petrolled his way into the history books
already, in the English in which *Gastarbeiters*
must henceforth beg for their revocable visas,
chanting a Brexit Festival chorus of National
Facts. Calais's not happy. Along the sea-coast,
migrants escaped from Britain, denounce our
charter deportations (in perfect English). Where
once Wyatt and Surrey, Wellington and Churchill,
waged eloquent war, we will again bulk-buy fags,
vomiting vino on our shoes. Safe on our shores
we shall sing: *We don't need no human rights
doing our business in our own backyard*

Toussaint, the most unhappy man of men!

Flat-Battery Bo, rusticated man's man!
Can you hear the lactating maids moaning
in the liberal groves of Chevening, while
you lie heeding no more than the two A4 sheet
briefings allotted by the Cum? Oh, miserable chief –
no time to scan them? Are you dead drunk,
or are you cackling in madman's chains, Sabisky's
eugenics? Your powers can't work against air,
earth and sky. Coronavirus breathes on the very wind
that brings the floods, yet you don't appear in mask,
with mop. You have great allies: Useless Eustace
exults lactic chicky washes, Bully Beef Patel delivers
agonies to her staff; but only you have rich
unconquerable love for your impenetrable mind.

Kjell Espmark

translated by Robin Fulton Macpherson

Mallarmé Calls Destruction His Beatrice

The room is empty and dark.
Tables and chairs, carpets and bookcases –
everything has been erased.
Just a mirror is allowed, in the background.
The tenant is satisfied to see
how the mirror disowns him,
reflecting only a cluster of stars.

Here existence has almost reached twelve.
Time has apparently foundered.
At 25 he's already in his later life
and can draw up its grammar
on a page of squared paper torn
from his red school-jotter.

The Book, his Divina Commedia,
the ultimate account of silence,
has, of course, erased itself
before it had time to begin.

It's a question of elimination.
What's left of the cup of coffee is an odour,
of the half-eaten croissant
the memory of a spot of grease
on the table already wiped out.
If anything could be thought of as left behind
it would be a triangular ashtray
full of the ash
that proves the world once existed.
What remains is the descent

of the dizzying spiral staircase
in what is only the smell of a cellar.
The thinning walls open into night.
Further and further down in the vertigo
that replaces the stairway. The low pressure
is immense. It's time to blow out the stars.
And then to erase oneself.
In the final darkness there are only words
reflecting themselves in a glitter.

Fugue

Tossing to and fro on my camp-bed,
coiled in the mosquito-net, running with sweat:
how many refugees can squeeze into
a single human? Without the whisky
I couldn't make it through to morning.

Right now: a mother and her little daughters
are creeping through a millet-field. She fears
the little one might start crying
and be strangled by the others.

News has spread that I'm a doctor
and the flow of refugees has veered my way –
children with bellies like water-bags
and women filleted inside-out.
How many of the desperate can I contain?

Right now: someone rests on dripping oars
while the patrol boat slides past in the dark.
And suddenly all is a searchlight blaze.

When I try to stitch together
the slashed belly of the one people

the other, sneaking shadows, threatens
to chop my hands off.
How much do we have to forgive?

Right now: they're wading through water
to avoid the sniffer dogs
and the cries of Kill! Kill! Their past
has just run them down.
I become a noisy refugee camp,
my brain a clutter of grey shacks
knocked together by hope and terror.
But the mutual hate is there too
like a latrine stench pervading my days.

How can the half of the world that's burning
be made new in the half that's spared?
The smoke takes our reservations.
The smoke is full of faces
which are only eyes and flight.

The Last Witch

In 1811
the last witch in Poland was burned
on a hill outside Reszel.
The town had burnt down four years before
and many could describe
how the spell flapped its way along the roofs.
The trial concluded beyond all doubt
that Barbara the witch had sent the fire.

Her bloodshot eyes in the pyre,
her crackling hair
and her screams for her children,
who'd been charitably removed,
all confirmed the wisdom of the verdict.

But then she fell silent, her gaze widened
as if she had seen heaven open.
The congregation backed off
with hearts as small as hazelnuts.

The fervent prayers of the priests
gradually calmed the crowd.
And a visiting doctor ensured
the infection burned like a TB victim's clothes

Her ashes drifted off through the years
and once again breathing was easy.
As if the smoke had taken with it
the congregation's inner darkness.

But the clouds, who'd seen most things,
memorized the composition of the ash.
Their well-travelled experience could be read.
The last witch is not the last.

Ezra Pound on the Galley Bench

How did I land up here
on a ship of stone that can't float
but is floating? A sweaty galley slave
in a crowd of dark rowers on the benches.
Most of their shoulders are coated with fish-scales.
What is my crime? The mumbling around me
implies I betrayed my country,
perhaps being complicit in a derided people
being burnt out of history.
Could it refer to Carthage? Who cares?
As if deceit and extermination were no more
than equations for human feelings.

The oldest slave, blind like Homer,
beats time on his drum: HEAVE HO, HEAVE HO!
The years pass like clouds of droplets.
When I stray into thoughts of my language
the whip whines on my back.

HEAVE HO, HEAVE HO!
Again and again the waves crash in,
the colour of grape flesh.
The skipper is, of course, Dionysus
As in Canto 11. (The rest of my book
seems condemned to a century of unreadability.)

It's hard to row with oars wreathed in vines.
Also the god himself – it's Mussolini –
Is adorned with vines round his bulk.
His Clara pouts a kiss at me.
The gulls over us, howling furies,
cast rapid shadows on the water.
Their eyes have the hard exactness
which my poetics seems to prescribe.
Allows me no revision whatever.

HEAVE HO, HEAVE HO! Instead of the smell of tar
There's the stench of beasts.
The guards skid on panther shit
and the growling competes with the hiss of the waves.
As if growling was my late style!
The words I find stink of ambush.

HEAVE HO, HEAVE HO! I'm plagued by the breath
of the panting oarsman behind me.
He keeps me in a spiteful chapter
where I look in vain for words of regret.

The Voice is Still Dressed for a Journey

The suitcase damaged during loading
then disgraced in a porch corner
travelled not on highways and byways
but through dusty years.
The light pulsing through the gash!

When it's eventually opened
(a grubby label mumbles Joan Murray)
the memory of the long dead owner,
condensed in letters, documents, poems,
now has a different voice.
The much too brief life
smuggled into a later century
has been bungled into its language.

Who was she?
And who has she become?
The flickering heart,
a valve struck by rheumatic fever,
that too has changed.

The unfinished plans, breathless, ward off
the completion seeking them out.
Let the hesitant star keep its night
and the outlined firmament its doubt.
Creation, those inky lines,
an out-of-work architect's dream
may well remain as a sketch.
Here we find completion in the incomplete.

Attila József

translated by Ágnes Lehóczky and Adam Piette

Dusk

This dusk, so sharp, so clear, it's made for me. Far off,
see how the structure, warp and weft of bare black boughs
with grace upholds the gravity of empty air.
As each and every subject's torn from every object;
they sink into themselves, perhaps they cease to be,
who knows? My gut feeling might have the right answer,
except that, like the dog that's bawled at by its master,
brooding over its feelings in the cold back yard,
it's howling at strangers, yet still won't breathe a word,
that's what gut-dog's like now. Can I do without him?
The only certainty: the mistakes that we make.
Lucky I lean on iambs: it's how kids learn to walk.
Only reason I can't pretend to be that child
is that I'd be too moody, bolshie, treacherous,
like everyone who's human (least that's what I think),
sly, mulish. And so? How could I possibly know?
Guy winks at me and says, hello, pretty boy,
another, lazy arse, you dodging work again?
your eyes as big as your belly, well, is that wrong?
A third tosses a coin, says, hope you'll muddle through,
I feel for you, I've been through hell as well, my friend,
another guy he nicks my junk, just coz he can.
A shove here, pull there, groping, poking, punching, croaking,
But none of them can see the hump there on my back,
the one I carry, like mad mother her foetus
which she'll give birth to, she thinks, sempiternal void.

Autumn, 1934

Our Poet and His Time Past

Here, here is my poem at long last,
Second line is this one, yes this.
Title, Our Poet and his Time Past,
puffs with plosive Ps and hisses.
Nothing floats inside, as if it were
made of air's dust, simply a sheer
nothingness.

Nothing floats inside, as if it were
something fabricated: this world.
It takes off towards its fate, soaring,
floating through all spacetime, wild
as the crashing sea and roar,
leaves in stormwind, dogs that whimper,
in wee hours curled.

I in my chair, top of this world,
of this Earth right under hot Sun,
solar system, prison, both whirl
steady through the constellations,
allness in the nothingnesses,
(inverse true in me I guess),
the idea shines.

Soul is space, if only I could
join up with big Mother Cosmos;
Basket to hot air balloon tied,
bind my soul's form to this body's.
This is not real, nor is it dream,
rather as they call it sublim-
ation of Das Es.

Come, do take a look around, guest,
You are working in this cosmos

same way as, and let's be honest,
solidarity in you does.
Leave it all behind. Now watch how
evening light brings the night low
down to its end.

See the stubble fields drenched in blood
stretched out to the far horizon.
Blood thickens to blue. Grass fades,
thins, browns, dies back, weeps and weakens.
On the sweet heaps livor mortis
softly sits and quietly spreads as
skies darken.

dedicated to Bertalan Hatvany, end of August 1937

The Loggers

The railway station bridge is shaking still,
though autumn's quiet breath begins to stir.
Dry timber logs are rumbling as they fall,
men throwing them from the dark railroad cars.

And if one settles, still the fallen stack
is silent. In trouble? I look scared stiff,
like always on the run, log on my back.
The little child I was is still alive.

The little kid I was is still alive,
while the grown-up wells up with tears – and yet
he chokes them back, and hums a song. Wind strives
to blow away his hat – he just won't let it.

Was it you, hard men, terrified me so,
tough loggers, lumberjacks I so admired?

Like stolen wood I'm carrying you as I go
through this homeless world of border guards and fear.

November, 1936.

Suburban Night

The light from the sideyard
slowly raises its net,
like a pothole in water mired,
our kitchen fills with twilight.

Silence, – the scrubbing brush, listless,
stirs almost, begins to crawl;
above it, a tiny chunk of wall is
wondering if it's time to fall.

In oily rags in the sky, the night
stops and sighs; sits down
on the outskirts of town.
Then sways on across the square, lights
up a little moon to shine so bright.

They rise like debris
the factories,
but nonetheless
in them a denser darkness,
groundwork to the silence.

On the windows of the textile mills
moonbeams flutter & fall,
the soft moonlight is the twill
of the yarn the looms unfurl,
till morning, while workers sleep still,
here, machines sullenly spin, enlace and seam
the weaving-women's dissolving dreams.

And further up, a cemetery of trade,
steel works, cement plant, screw factory.
Family crypts that echo eerily.
These factories are like guards of the mystery
of a sombre resurrection.
A cat scratches at the metal fence
& the superstitious night watchman
sees a ghost, a sudden flash of light, –
the beetle-backed dynamos
shine coolly in the night.

A train whistles.

A copper on the road, a mumbling worker,
a comrade with leaflets & flyers
hurries by, sniffs the air
leaning forward like a dog,
& like a cat, ears pricked, fast
glances back, snaking round each lamppost.

Stale light from a pub doorway cast,
the windows puking puddles out;
stifled lantern swings & gasps,
solitary dayworker waits up all night.
The innkeeper dozes, gulps for air,
grins & snarls at the bare wall,
seethes his way up the lush stairwell, cries "Up the revolution!" in the hall.

Like cold smelt ore, the lapping
waters solidify, stiffening.
The wind, like a stray dog, passes over,
its huge tongue lolling into the river,
gulping down water, drinking it in.
Straw beds like small rafts swim
silently by on the night currents of the waters.

The depot's a stranded ark,
the foundry an iron craft,
the iron-founder's dreams they make
a red baby from iron casts.

Everything is wet, everything hangs heavy.
A clear map of poverty's countries
is drawn by mould's unlovely
hand. And there on barren pastures,
rags on ragged grasses & waste paper.
How it'd long to move, heart jittery!
But too tired to even start to…

Damp & sticky copy of your breath,
flapping dirty sheets to death,
o night!
You hang roped up to the sky,
threadbare muslin, hanging high,
like grief, on life, o night!
Night of the poor! Be coal for me,
burn and glow your fire on me,
melt the iron that is inside
into the solid anvil that abides,
into the clinking clanking hammer,
into blades that swish to victory & honour,
o night!

The night is heavy, the night is dark & cold.
I'm heading to bed too, my brothers.
Let no anguish settle on the soul.
Let no worm our flesh devour.

1932

Lutz Seiler

translated by Stefan Tobler

spoilheap glow

we're talking physics here: incidents, apparent lifelessness,
mineshaft temples suddenly purple; *spoilheap glow*
was a drinkable liquor, duty-free
                for cave-dwellers, but:
'on Labour Day, out on the street'.

              and evenings
the acrylic jacket, in the stalls
for stone-age operettas, cattle
in the outbuilding, evenings
the Easter bunny's twitching; a bundle

hanging draughty on a beam compare
to rabbits, mange-eaten: when first
your feet lose their sight, then
the slow vanishing of your eyes; white

like how in my lamp's cone
survival leaps in
furs, furrows, down
country roads'
inner walls: you

  loved it when
the sheep undulated, their lousy
twitching in their sleep, the little
spasm in *Glück auf!* – it all

reminds you of something
under shavings, under-

mined a wind
   at eye-level
rises out of the past; with every look
the sides are changing, every blink is digging
   you a cave in time

summing up

   you stand like a branch
your steps all wooden
   since the age of short trousers
in the shadow: a third one.

   a forward bend
it finds its place
   at a quicker pace

it rises up
   it passes soon
going down the road. only a sudden

   staticky hiss
whatever the frequency
so not with standing
you lean into your steps

Felizetti's garden

walking falls ill
with darkened grounds
& water from laughter & whistling
like crying like phlegm

on teeth plaque broken sentences
pierced ears I hate

the woman her hand on her eyes
brings the dark safely over
   down into her over-dark breath
   through the fencing

around our garden her weathered child
drifts with stones in his blood with
bird crap of hair tufts of
   the sheer stench over the garden
fence against the Felizetti

house stones and curses
smashed, the roof the
child jumps over & splits like
ice on pig bellies
   his spitty breath
tolls out in winter to the furnaces
in the villages' sky, utterly damned

you leave, Felizetti,
from our shame half a sentence
       half a child
with sugared lips you
   step into the tent of light above
the fields into the public body
of the forest a *magic pop-up lark* but

whatever in the root shadow of your trip
we kicked from your heels old Felizetti
whirled straight up to God

scissors knives and matches

I was walking up to my knees with the current, so
corpses overtook me, a soft
white shoulder bashed
horizontal into the taut
throat of my knee I swayed forward,

side, together, tap with a water
waltzing step to let
a great dead swimmer slip
lengthwise past me but straight
away another water-head
was pushing between my legs, so

I stumbled, I did, no, not quite
I danced that next
quarter twist of my leg to the left,
back, side, together, tap
the dead, their way free, continued
stiff as pigs who swim between islands
down the boulevard, where to, I

don't know it was raining I was dancing in
the giant heaving swell until
the evening threw down a shimmer for scissors
knives and matches
under thinly glazed fontanelles

Roelof Ten Napel

translated by Judith Wilkinson

About Rain

Where does the rain fall in poems?
In the past, one Argentinian said.
For him, the rain fell in a village
that no longer existed, he heard
the voice of his father, suddenly
no longer dead. Rain reminds you of rain,
it repeats itself instantly.
(Did you feel something? You raise
the palm of your hand. You try to
be touched there – in what way?)
Rain is nothing but its own, constant
rehearsal. You stand in all rains at once,
your hand tentatively raised.
That gesture isn't yours, it was simply
passed on to you.
Meanwhile not a second has passed.

The Other Thing

How slender my wrist feels, like a broomstick
when I grab hold of it, grab hold of *me*, gripping
my bone there. I'm always still that object
too. Object, instrument? Or not?
My body: the thought that I keep skipping over,
that only grabs my attention when it falters.
The quiet weight of a centre,
by my eyes when I look, high up in my chest
when I move, or hug someone.

My body seems to be what conceals itself
in my actions, follows me like a horizon.
Not *this* horizon, but that constant depth
that can't be erased,
keeps receiving new views.
A moving window.

Just Shy of a Ritual

Switching on all the lights in the evening, one by one,
and knowing what guise the room will take on.
In what light is your face your real face,
in what light do you see the faces of those you know?
Maybe in the morning I picture those dear to me
differently from in the evening. What changes

when I turn off the lights inside? Our memory
knows our honest maps and floor plans,
our desire knows which spots
should have adjoined.
They retain what didn't happen, in the same house —
who we almost were,
in almost the same place.

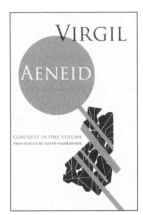

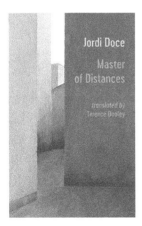

Recent translations from Shearsman Books

Notes on Contributors

SERENA ALAGAPPAN received her A.B. in comparative literature and creative writing from Princeton University in 2020, and has recently graduated with an MSt in World Literatures in English at Oxford as a Rhodes Scholar. Her poems have appeared in *The London Magazine, The American Journal of Poetry, the Colorado Review, Stand Magazine, the Oxford Review of Books, the Cambridge Review of Books, West Trade Review, Bear Review*, and elsewhere. She is a recipient of the 2022 New Poets Prize and her pamphlet *Sensitive to Temperature* was published by Smith|Doorstop this year.

WENDY ALLEN's work has appeared in *Poetry Wales, Ambit, Poetry Ireland Review* and *The North*. Her debut pamphlet, *Plastic Tubed Little Bird*, was published earlier this year by Broken Sleep. She will begin a PhD in Creative Writing at Manchester Metropolitan University in October 2023, and is currently supported by Arts Council England with her current writing project on Barbara Hepworth and the female body.

MARK BYERS is an academic at Newcastle specialising in late modernist poetry. His first book was on Charles Olson (OUP 2018) and he is currently editing the letters of Tom Raworth. Some of his recent poems have appeared in small magazines such as *Amberflora* and *The Projectionist's Playground*.

ELIZABETH CHADWICK PYWELL was awarded the Northern Writers' Debut Award for Poetry in 2022. Her pamphlet, *Breaking (Out)* was published by Selcouth Station Press, and *Unknown* by Stairwell Press. She has featured in journals including *Fourteen Poems, New Welsh Review, Spelt, Strix, The Alchemy Spoon, Ink Sweat and Tears and Impossible Archetype*, has longlisted for the Leeds Poetry Prize and Mslexia Women's Poetry Competition, and shortlisted for the Ironbridge Festival Prize.

PETER DUKES teaches at the University of Westminster in media and visual arts. Work has appeared in *Magma, Long Poem Magazine,* and *The New River* amongst other publications, and is nearing the end of a practice-led PhD in visual-material poetry.

DAVID DUMOURIEZ was born, has lived a bit, and will probably die.

KJELL ESPMARK (1930–2022) was Professor of Comparative Literature at Stockholm University (1978–1995), member of The Swedish Academy (from 1981) and Nobel Committee Chairman (1988–2004). His impressive output of poems, fiction and scholarly works earned him many European awards and his work has been translated into over twenty languages. Five of his poetry collections in English translation have been published, three by Marick Press in the USA, and two by Shearsman.

MARIE-LOUISE EYRES received her MFA in poetry from MMU in 2020 after receiving a brain tumour diagnosis in 2018. Her poems have twice been longlisted in the National Poetry Competition and have placed in the Bridport, Bedford, Ginkgo AONB and Live Canon prizes. Recent work can be found in editions of *Stand, Agenda, Modern Poetry in Translation, Poetry Magazine, Portland Review* and elsewhere. Her chapbooks include *Wolf Encounters* (Maverick Duck), *Seed – found poetry from The Great Gatsby* (Alien Buddha), *When we lived in LA* (Alien Buddha) and the upcoming *Into a Salt Marsh*

Heart (Finishing Line). Originally from London, she lives in California with her family.

DOMINIC FISHER was co-editor of Bristol-based *Raceme* magazine, which recently published its final issue. His second collection *A Customised Selection of Fireworks*, appeared last year from Shoestring Press, and his first was published in 2019 by The Blue Nib. He is also a member of the Bristol performance group the IsamBards.

MARK GOODWIN is the author of a number of collections, including three from Shearsman: *Else, Back of A Vast* and *The House at Out*. A fourth, *At*, is in development.

AMLANJYOTI GOSWAMI has written two widely reviewed books of poetry, *Vital Signs* and *River Wedding*, both published by Poetrywala. His poems have been published in journals and anthologies around the world including *Poetry, The Poetry Review, Rattle, Penguin Vintage* and *Sahitya Akademi*. His poems have also appeared on street walls in Christchurch, exhibitions in Johannesburg, an e-gallery in Brighton and buses in Philadelphia. He has reviewed poetry for *Modern Poetry in Translation* and has read in various places, including New York, Delhi, Chandigarh, Bangalore and Boston. He grew up in Guwahati and lives in Delhi.

JOHN GREENING is author of over twenty collections, including *Selected Poems 1977–2022* (Baylor University Press, ed. Kevin Gardner), *The Interpretation of Owls* (Baylor UP), *The Silence* (Carcanet, 2019) and the recent pamphlets *The Giddings* (Mica, 2021) and *Omniscience* (Broken Sleep, 2022). He has edited Edmund Blunden's memoir, *Undertones of War*, the poetry of Geoffrey Grigson and Iain Crichton Smith (Carcanet) as well as anthologies on music, sheds, rubbish, country houses and Englishness (the last two with Kevin Gardner). His essays, *Vapour Trails*, appeared in 2020 and there is a further selection in *A High Calling* from Broken Sleep, due June 2023. A new collection of his Goethe translations, *Nightwalker's Song*, has just been published by Arc.

FINN HAUNCH has also been published in *Ink, Sweat & Tears, bind, Dark Mountain*, and has work in the recent, final issue of *Raceme*.

NEIL HOSKINS works in publishing. His writing has appeared in the UK, Ireland and Canada. He is currently at work on a novella in verse around the life and times of the electric lightbulb inventor, Joseph Swan.

ATTILA JÓZSEF (1905–1937) was one of the most important Hungarian poets of the 20th century. His books, among others, in Hungarian are *A szépség koldusa* (1922); *Nem én kiáltok* (1925); *Nincsen apám se anyám* (1929); *Külvárosi éj* (1932); *Medvetánc* (1934); *Nagyon fáj* (1936); *József Attila összes versei és válogatott írásai* (1938); *József Attila összes verse* (1950); *József Attila összes versei* (1984). His poems in English have been published in *Poems* (Danubia Book Company, 1956); *Selected Poems and Texts* (Carcanet Press, 1973); *Perched on Nothing's Branch,* trans. by Peter Hargitai (White Pine Press, 1978); *Winter Night: Selected Poems of Attila József*, trans. by John Batki (Oberlin College Press, 1997); *Poems and Fragments* (Argentum/Cardinal Press, 1999); *The Iron-Blue Vault: Selected Poems*, trans. by Zsuzsanna Ozsváth and Fredrick Turner (Bloodaxe Books, 2000); *Attila József: Sixty Poems*, trans. by Edwin Morgan (Mariscat, 2001); *Attila József: Selected Poems* (Universe, 2005); *A Transparent Lion: Selected Poems of Attila József,* trans. by Michael Castro and Gabor G. Gyukics (Green Integer, 2006).

Fiona Larkin's pamphlets are *Vital Capacity* (Broken Sleep, 2022) and *A Dovetail of Breath* (Rack Press, 2020). Her debut collection, *Rope of Sand*, appears with Pindrop Press this year. Highly commended in the Forward Prizes, she manages innovative projects with Corrupted Poetry; their next event forms part of the Bloomsbury Festival in October.

Peter Larkin's most recent collection, *If Trees Allay an Earth Retrialling*, appeared from Shearsman Books earlier this year, his seventh with the press.

Ágnes Lehóczky's UK poetry collections include *Carillonneur* (Shearsman Books, 2014) and *Swimming Pool* (Shearsman, 2017). *Lathe Biosas, or on Dreams & Lies*, part of a larger project, was published by Crater Press in 2023. She has three full poetry collections in Hungarian, published in Budapest. She is also the author of a monograph on the poetry of Ágnes Nemes Nagy. She has co-edited several major international anthologies, most recently *The World Speaking Back to Denise Riley* (Boiler House, 2017) with Zoë Skoulding. She is Senior Lecturer in Creative Writing, Programme Convenor of the MA in Creative Writing and Director of the Centre for Poetry and Poetics at the University of Sheffield.

Rupert M Loydell is Senior Lecturer in the School of Writing and Journalism at Falmouth University, the editor of *Stride* magazine, and contributing editor to *International Times*. He is a widely published poet whose most recent collection is *The Age of Destruction and Lies* (Shearsman Books, 2023). He has edited anthologies for Salt, Shearsman and KFS, written for academic journals, and contributed to books about David Lynch, Brian Eno and Industrial music.

Valeria Melchioretto is the author of *Podding Peas, The End of Limbo* and *1348 & Other Equations*.

Eliza O'Toole has a PhD from the University of Essex where she walked among experimental poets of note. Her first collection of poetry, *The Dropping of Petals*, was published in 2021 by Muscaliet Press. Muscaliet is publishing her second collection, *The Formation of Abscission Layers*, this year.

John Phillips is a Cornishman now living in Slovenia. Among his many publications are *The Shape of Faith* from Shearsman Books (2017).

Adam Piette is Professor of Modern Literature at the University of Sheffield and is the author of *Remembering and the Sound of Words: Mallarmé, Proust, Joyce, Beckett* (OUP), *Imagination at War: British Fiction and Poetry, 1939–1945* (Macmillan), *The Literary Cold War, 1945 to Vietnam* (Edinburgh UP), with Mark Rawlinson. He also co-edits the international poetry journal *Blackbox Manifold* with Alex Houen. His poetry collection *Nights as Dreaming* was published by Constitutional Information in 2023.

Amber Rollinson is a poet and artist based in Bristol. She is a graduate of the MSt Creative Writing at Oxford and has been published in various publications including *Neon, Stand, Mslexia,* and *Channel*. Her debut pamphlet *Somewhere, Looking* was published by Broken Sleep Books in 2022, and a second is forthcoming from Erro Press.

D'or Seifer lives in Limerick, where she runs the Lime Square Poets series. Her work has appeared in *Skylight 47, The Banyan Review, Abridged, Ink Sweat & Tears* and

Romance Options anthology. Recently she read at the New Writers Showcase at Cúirt Festival of Literature and on the Eat the Storms podcast.

Poet, novelist and essayist **LUTZ SEILER** was born in Gera, Thuringia, in 1963 and today lives in Wilhelmshorst, near Berlin, and in Stockholm. After an apprenticeship in construction, he worked as a carpenter and bricklayer. His writing has won many prizes, including the Leipzig Book Fair Prize, the Ingeborg Bachmann and the German Book Prize, and been translated into twenty-five languages. His prize-winning second novel *Star 111*, his volume of non-fiction *In Case of Loss* and the poetry collection *Pitch & Glint* are published in English translation in 2023 by And Other Stories.

NATALIE SHAW has been described as 'wonderfully bananas' by the TLS. *Dirty Martini* was published in January this year by Broken Sleep, following *Oh be quiet* with Against the Grain.

ROBERT SHEPPARD's poems in this issue come from *British Standards*, the third part of a trilogy of sonnet sequences that includes *The English Strain* (Shearsman, 2021) and *Bad Idea* (Knives Forks and Spoons, 2021).

Born in Belém, Brazil, to English and Swiss parents, **STEFAN TOBLER** is a translator and the founder of the publishing house And Other Stories. Authors he has translated include Clarice Lispector, Raduan Nassar, Antônio Moura and Arno Geiger. His own poetry has been published in *Shearsman* and other magazines. He grew up in northern Brazil and southern England, and has now made his home in the Dark Peak.

JUDI SUTHERLAND is an English poet currently living in Ireland, and her work currently reflects her interest in the history and geography of both countries. She has published two pamphlets to date: *The Ship Owner's House* (Vane Women Press, 2018) and *Following Teisa* (The Book Mill, 2021). Journal publications have been in *New Statesman, Oxford Poetry, The North, The High Window,* and *Poetry Ireland Review*.

ROELOF TEN NAPEL, born in 1993, is a Dutch poet, novelist and essayist. His most recent collection, *Dagen in huis*, was awarded De Grote Poëzieprijs, Holland's most prestigious poetry prize. The Dutch newspaper *De Volkskrant* has called him 'the most exciting poet of his generation.' The poems translated here are from *Dagen in Huis* (Hollands Diep, Amsterdam 2021).

JUDITH WILKINSON is a British poet and award-winning translator, living in Groningen. She is currently translating Roelof ten Napel, with a view to a *Selected Poems*. Recent collections include Hanny Michaelis, *In an Unguarded Moment, Selected Poems*, Shoestring, 2022, and *In Desert* (her own poetry), Shoestring, 2021. Wilkinson has translated many Dutch and Flemish poets, including Hagar Peeters, Toon Tellegen, Miriam Van hee and Menno Wigman.